Gallery Books
Editor Peter Fallon

THE ASH AND THE OAK AND
THE WILD CHERRY TREE

Kerry Hardie

THE ASH
AND THE OAK
AND THE WILD
CHERRY TREE

Gallery Books

The Ash and the Oak and the Wild Cherry Tree
is first published
simultaneously in paperback
and in a clothbound edition
on 9 June 2012.

The Gallery Press
Loughcrew
Oldcastle
County Meath
Ireland

www.gallerypress.com

ISBN 978 1 85235 534 0 *paperback*
     978 1 85235 535 7 *clothbound*

A CIP catalogue record for this book
is available from the British Library.

Contents

Being Here, Now

A suede-coloured bull, two cows and a calf in the pasture.
A blue seep under spring's green sting.

Swallows flicking about on the face of the river.
And swifts, their cutlass-play that cleaves the air.

This day — a round place of clean brightness,
a drop of rain laid on a pleated leaf.

for my brother, Paddy,
who died in Delhi
on 15 January 2012, aged forty-seven,
and for Lu and their little sons,
Ned and Thomas

Sixty

Everyone is slowly going home.
The shadow of the pine
lies stretched and sprawled across the trodden sands.
The waterline creeps close.

I am watching my husband grow old —
the stoop in the lines of his bones,
the hesitant note in his gait
where once there was ease and strut.

This mirror his form holds to mine
is not how I want things to be.
It cancels the contract of life,
it stifles our birth-howl with clay.

But everyone is slowly going home.
The shadow of the pine
lies stretched and sprawled across the trodden sands.
The waterline creeps close.

April 2013

[signature]

*for a great lady on her
great birthday*

Visiting

Sometimes these days I fold my hands and sit quietly,
a good child.

I think of hair ribbons and fear.
An upright chair beside a half-closed door.

Dishes and bosoms. Voices.
Closed things
laid out and looked at, lives decided.

⌇

Why would I want to belong
anywhere?

Otters

Fucshia flowers weighted with rain.
Black bog-flesh, sodden and dense.
Nowhere to go but within.

Last night I was far out at sea.
Winged otters gambolled black rocks.
Cresting waves crashed, then slid back.

Now the rain comes, the rain goes.
All day the otters stay close.
The fucshia flowers hang, small red stabs.

I sit at the window and think
of the body gone back to the earth,
of the end of myself to myself.

But the otters with wings come and go.
They are marvellous, fearless and bright.
And I shine and I shine and I shine.

Letter from the Old World

for my brother Paddy

The rain has stopped.
Someone is moving
sheep on the road.
Blue shadows shift
like a hung wash on the mountains.
They follow the clouds.

How is New York?
The shops and flats and people?

Seán is digging out the winter spinach.
I hear the scrape of steel on stones.
It is May, a wet Sunday in May —
the air, greenish and moist.
Sweet rocket splays
its mauve fronds on the air.
                         Yesterday
I placed its flowers in the blue glass vase
and set them on that bookcase that we use
for gloves and keys and mislaid things.
I catch its perfume as I turn the stairs
and trail the sweetness with me down the hall.
Sweet rocket, sometimes called dame's violet,
carried here by Huguenots who fled from France.
Slips packaged up in moss. What do hands fumble for
when dread comes calling?
Ah, but there's nothing in the world to match
this lush, damp garden in the damp, green light.
Not much in flower yet — all grows out and up.
The cow parsley's waist-high, the nettles rise.

For me, the world is well because the pigeon's call
lets slaughter sleep.

Those Huguenots —
their flight-route signalled by these unprized flowers
that rise by paths and ditches everywhere.
All roadsides in the world are unmarked graves
for those that strife or famine dispossessed.
Green places, where the spent lay down
like bundled clothes too worn to wear.

I can smell cattle on the wind now, a hot stench,
they bellow in the field behind the ash.

The Satin Gown

On the back of the door a black satin gown,
blooming red roses, passionate as blood.

These days, this marriage house,
the quiet hours of passage.
Wind soughing in the ash trees all night through.

The torn gown hangs there on the wooden peg.
Cheap wine, wet streets and rented rooms.
Cigarettes and borrowed clothes
and falling in and out of sex like love.
Sometimes I seek its slither on my naked skin,
like lifting off the white paint with a fingernail —
underneath, the dirty, gaudy colours.

Waning

Some days you wake in July,
by evening it feels like September.

Yesterday was August all day,
the thistledown drifting the roads.

Just the same, it was hard to trust life.
All that I love is alive and already dying.

Hoarding old bones — the splinters of saints —
would be saner. In the fields

they were reaping, the sounds drawing closer,
then circling away down the meadow.

How can we love
when love must watch life cease to live?

How can we not
when downy seeds blow the ripe roads?

How We Carry On Pretending

I am that woman in the summer frock —
bright words and laughter, the odd sweeping gesture
towards that mansion that her mind's eye sees,
all dressed grey stone and ordered march of windows.

Instead there is a small, tired house,
half derelict, and anyone can see
the forked crack gaping in the gable end,
the ivy pushing from inside the rooms,

levering a way through empty frames,
reaching its scabby arms towards the light.
She is ridiculous, I turn away,
embarrassed in the face of such denial.

Yet I still talk as though my roof is sound,
as though my bed is made up with fresh linen,
far from this nest of leaks and drips and noises,
of rotting beams and slates that split and fall.

If I could leave off listening for the laughter
of visitors who peer and stretch and mock
then I might hear the singing in the roof beams,
the strange, resplendent voices I once knew,

might watch white stars through my own ragged rafters,
unnumbered galaxies the daylight hides.

Self Portrait

I fear the dark bird
that sits in the rustling
leaves of my tree,

the dark bird that's always
waiting to plunge
on the mortal crouch of myself.

I fear its cruel eye,
its blood-rusted beak.
Its talons drip history.

                ~

I am the dark bird
that sits in the leaves,
neither shifting nor blinking.

I am the raw flesh
that's hunched at the roots
ensnared in my fear.

But who is this tree,
its great branches singing and sighing,
sheltering a raptor,

shielding its prey?

The Ash and the Oak and the Wild Cherry Tree

All day the trees were talking behind my back,
telling those tales about silence,
how it comes when the leaves are gone,
when the wind doesn't move around in the sky,
when the snow lies.

I remember how my mother
would stand beside the window
watching for the weather to come right.
I remember horizons,
her skirts bunched in my hands.

I need the trees to tell that other story,
the one that's murmurous with wind and leaves,
to witness for me in the way I crave.
She is old now.
She sways
though no wind blows.

Waking Up

I took the cutters out of my pocket,
drew the long knife from my stocking,
laid them on the table. Then I opened my eyes.

The weather was blowing across the skylight.
I sat up, threw back the bedclothes,
stepped onto the wooden boards.

That was the day starting. Vulnerable. Open.

Later there was the wide, grey estuary,
the sands, the windy light, the seabirds calling.
The skies were cities that formed and dispersed.

Away in the distance the pup was clearing the gulls.
Right under my feet the suck of the watery sands,
the ooze and wormcasts squirming between my toes.

I was a dot, a tiny concentration
of blood and bone and intelligence
moving about

under all that vastness. Isn't it strange?
At once so particular
and so enormous.

Satnav for Melo, Dying

Hic Finis Chartae Viaeque —
Here the map ends. The known ends.
And written on old maps
beyond the land's drawn boundaries:
Here be monsters.

Maps:
how they were needed
for navigation, for military adventures;
after defeat
for the confiscation of lands.

Maps:
how they are needed
for lives, futures, notions of well-being;
to keep the fear confined,
the boundaries sealed.

Hic Finis Chartae Viaeque —
Here the map ends. The known ends.
So, run the boat out for the old adventure.
Risk beyond all charted waters,
ride the glittering seas.

October

The world is a small red fox.
The light is a golden goose
laying eggs in the pumpkin patch.

The red fox moves through the grass.
He snuffles about in the wrinkled leaves
on the scent of the golden goose.

But the golden goose will drown in the night
of the deep black rains of November.
The little red fox will shrivel and starve,
his white bones will lie in the fields.

Nothing is Simple

1

Look, friend god, I can write,
the plaster has gone from my arm,
my hand can once more hold the pen,
can record how the meadow grass shines,
how the bull roars in Daly's barn,
how the crows climb the pure, clear air.
Friend god, are you living inside us
as people sometimes claim?
Are you the eye that is reading these words,
the hand that is writing them down?
Are you the light in the grass,
the sex that is roaring the bull,
the crows, and the pure, clear air,
the glass-shards that turn in my wrist?
But if you are pain, who is friend?
And if you are friend, why the pain?

2

Jim was night-hunting. Alone.
Making noises like a broken thing,
injured and close to death.
It drew the foxes.

Our cat stalked out of the dark.
He said she was lucky.
Most men would have shot her.
Something to kill.

And this is also god.

Fruit Net

It always begins the same way.
The young pup goes rooting
down there where the whitethorns
funnel the gloom.

A crouch and a pounce.
Something is thrashing about in the net.
There must be a way through I haven't found
where songbirds — blackbirds, thrushes — go
to pock the autumn's leavings.
Then, panicked by the pup, they rush full-flight
into the drapes and foldings of the net.

It's quiet now, the wet air stirs
the wind chimes in an empty tree.

I catch the trapped thrush in my hand
and, sliding scissor blades beneath the down,
cut strand on strand.

The bird strains and a fresh blood marks
the soft grey stuff of breast, the mottled throat.

Then suddenly its head turns and it strikes,
then strikes again, oblique, the angle poor,
eye fixed, beak wide, an empty wrenching gape
like those old tales where tongues were torn away
to silence witness.

It stills, I still. It rests within my hands,
its life intense as mine.

The last strand gives.
                            A wing-rush
and it's gone into the dusk.

The Emigrant's Photo

for Hughie O'Donoghue

This is the one who will leave, has already gone,
has stood in the open door
hearing his thoughts like a voice —
You will never see this again.

And he's paused, and a mist has come down on his mind:
he's looked at the yellow leaves in the grass,
the rain lying down on the tussocky field,
the cows nosing over the gate.

Stand over there —
He has stood by the net of the thorn.
Take off your hat —
It's been thrown on the grass behind.

He's strong, his chest is too strong
for his jacket, his strength
is bursting its buttons, shooting its sleeves,
pushing its pockets awry.

He lives warm and alive with death
but listens, intent, inside life which will sear
the skin of his hands and the soles of his feet
when the leathers are gone from his boots.

He will weep, drink, weep, drink again,
having flesh that will teach
how to live, how to die,
who it is who's doing either.

And the light which made this moment of him?
This light already reclaims him.

From Time to Time Red Dog Shows Up in the Forest

I don't know his name.
'Dog,' I call out to his presence.

My voice makes a bell in the woods
which are vague with gnats and thick light.

He steps from behind the dense trees
and stands there, attentive, tongue lolling.

Great cauliflower-domed seed heads of hogweed
tower the overgrown path.

Then he's off.
Dogness of dog

into woodness of woods.
My feet make small sounds in the silence.

Pyrenean Round

The sun is the shaman,
the air's thick and humming,
the bright trees are flowing,
the light's in the dance.

The sky's drifting higher,
the shaman is failing,
the slopes are red-burning,
the light cannot hold.

The mountains grow stronger,
the silence is listening,
the shaman lies dying,
the empty air thins.

The raven has spoken,
the pledge can't be broken,
the silence is rattling
the shaman's grey bones.

The sun is the shaman,
the air's lithe and dancing,
the trees are bright-leafing,
the light's flecked with gold.

Dutchmen's Trousers

i.m. Shelagh Jacob

She'd search the wide sky for a break in the cloud,
some rent in the grey expanse.
'There,' she would tell me, 'just enough blue
to make a Dutchman his trousers.'

All afternoon it promised more rain,
then colour blew in from the back of the sea,
and I knew she was up in the sky with the wind,
wrenching the storm-clouds apart.

I was wearing no shoes, I had to take care
because of the sea holly, sharp in the dunes,
though not the late heartsease, purple and yellow,
those colours the skin takes from bruising.

The sea holly's leaves are the washed jade of water,
its spikes are as fierce and relentless as grief,
its blooms are the blue of the cloth that they used
for those storybook, baggy Dutch trousers.

Heartsease is the herbalist's name for wild pansy,
which she never trusted — their bright, clever faces —
she tried not to look too hard at the world,
at the people with thorns in their eyes.

But heartsease has petals as soft as fine silk,
and ragged blue trousers come patched with grey sky,
and needles of sea holly sew a deep seam
through the dunes and the wave-wash of lace.

Porcelain Man

He always set porcelain
outside the shop
to pull in the women,
pricing it low —
a few pence for a plate —
the temptation
they allowed themselves,
he said —

Now — watching you —
up on that stool,
how you lift down a plate,
stroke
the blue lozenges
pressed on the rim,
polish the garlands,
dust off the centre,

I'm shooting my arm out
over the years,
I reach for the plate,
touch him again —
his slung hips
in his faded jeans,
his brown curls, and he always
loved women.

Sky

After the storm had done its worst
the light crept out and stretched
and spread across the yard,

uncurled the tight crouch
of the frightened sky, unfolded
a blue sash upon a wind

that cleared the cloud
and let the sun soft-splash
the fuchsia's fallen heaps of blood-red flowers.

Negation

on seeing a painting by Hanne Borchgrevink

The house has no windows
and there is no door.
The path that leads from it
falls out of the frame.
The house has no chimney
to push out thin plumes.
The sky has no clouds.

The house stands
on a dark field.
It haunts where the mind
is dumb.

Who has painted
this refugeless journey?
Who is it who denies us
comfort in our deepest places?

Hennessy's

for Maya Homburger and Barry Guy

They're in some foreign capital
performing Bach.
I climb their gate and walk their land,
through stubble, past great trees,
their rebuilt house, an ironed dress
laid ready on the bed.

The old house squats in the new house.
The old moon squats in the new moon.
And the hawk's plunge through the August dusk,
and the rabbit's blooded scream.

Envying No One

There's two young ones, a dog and two children
down by the lake.
The toddler's on the jetty with the father,
throwing sticks for the dog.
She has the babe on her back.

What a heap of responsibility
to carry through life.
And the lake shining and dancing.
And the world blowing green with the morning,

and I, setting off on my stride —
as lonely and happy
as one of those Zen solitaries
walking the earth, making poems

about roads and snow
and coughing and drinking and making poems.

Grace

At the station
the rain is over,
it is before the rain.

Sky, then ash trees, then
hawthorn, rowan, elder.
Cow parsley, wild carrot, chervil,
all in full flower.
The scent dredges down through the wet air
like icing sugar from a sifter.
It dissolves on touch with the warm earth,
runs off in puffs
like breath.
Sunday morning. People waiting: the farmers
in caps, their wives in new dresses, their young
sporting trainers. They stand around,
inside this invisible fragrance.
There is something
unearthly about it. Like the fragrance
from the body of a saint.
Flowering grasses grow between the sleepers.
Rain comes again. Not cold, whitening the sky.
Curling fronds of opening leaves
stretching in the straight, clean rain.
And the quiet people, waiting.

Happy Endings

We are the children you settled at play
with our buckets and spades in the sun.
There was a plan, but it went with the tide;
everyone ended up too drunk to stand,
our shoes floated off and we grizzled with cold
and the evening light pearled the wavering line
where the sea took the edge off the land.

Timing

A man died in the valley today.
I can see the house if I lean far out,
throwing the window wide to the lamb's loud bleating.

He had gone on
going on
dying all winter.

I wouldn't wait and die in the spring
when the darkness lifts off the world
like an old quilt,

wouldn't wait for this bursting light,
this insistence of birds and lambs.
The new-opened door
slammed shut in my face.

Perhaps he had to.
Only then, finally to know
it was beyond him, keeping up, completely
beyond him.

When the death news ran we looked at the ground
where our feet were planted. Then off somewhere.
Between two trees.
At the patched door on a stone shed.
At the post van, disappearing.

Modomnoc's Bees

died c. 550 AD

When Modomnoc wanted sainthood he took himself off to Wales and sought out David. David let him look after his bees.

No one cares anymore about all those years spent in Wales, but after he'd dipped his fingers in David's holiness Modomnoc came back to Ireland and dabbled about in more local mud. Hence his modest hermitage at Tobroughney, not a million miles from where I live.

Perhaps he came back on a ship, perhaps he stepped into a skin-covered boat that skidded the waves. Stories change shape with the teller. Whichever it was, his bees followed.

There are distant descendants of Modomnoc's most faithful disciples buzzing around in the sunshine, stroking the sex organs of tulips and magnolia and jonquils, all open together on account of the long hard winter we've just put behind us. Dandelions, celandines and forget-me-nots wait for attention. Desires less flaunted but no less urgent.

Which makes me think it's time I left off sitting at my desk, went outside and sowed a few seeds that will flower with the summer. Flowers to excite and arouse. Perhaps after all it was God that Modomnoc wanted. Sainthood was only a bi-product, like honey.

Away from Home

In Amsterdam the high geese stirred our sleep.
Their journeying filled our woken selves with longing.
The belling voices up there in the night.
The wavering squadrons, their vast, empty flight.

Pandora's Last Shake of the Box

for Hana el Degham

It was just an old box —
so who could have known
of the hatch of bald crows
and the thin scrawny moon
that would scrape the sky clean,
then throw itself out
through the door of the dawn,
where the Palm Sunday donkey
still trots through the streets?

But the shouting rose up
and the blackened birds flew
straight into the towers,
and no one could see
through the billowing smoke
how the donkey ran on,
how it circled the world
with a cross on its back
and a crescent moon caught
on its velvety ears,
how it brayed that the words
were given for all
of the peoples who walk
down below in the dust.

Protecting the Buds

It was time.
We bound the young apple trees,
looping the fine black thread
from twig to angled twig.

A low grey day. Winter, half turning,
waited on spring toiling after.
The moist air doused thought,
the bullfinches sat in the thorn hedge, waiting.

We knew that the snare was only defence,
hardly more than an incantation —
that it left the trees barely webbed,
their downy grey buds still presenting.

With their black caps
and their armoured beaks,
the pillagers sat impassive.
Their beauty and their fierce intention.

A helplessness.
It was like watching children,
their own bright, fatal thoughts
ranged round about them.

The Sunfish or Common Mola

in the Natural History Museum, Dublin

After thirty years I am back, visiting,
staring into the round glass eye of a fish
at once so weird and so enormous it's astounding
that the word 'common' forms part of its name.

It's here on the right in the same place.
This fish, called a sunfish or common mola,
has been gliding effortlessly down this gallery
since it was hauled from Lough Swilly in 1888,

the date someone wrote on its label
(though the scholarly hand that made the identification,
not being stuffed, mounted, touched up from time to time,
will long since have crumbled away).

I used to swim in Lough Swilly myself.
Had I known this gigantic dinner plate
(with its stubby fins extended, taller than I am)
might be waiting to rise from the depths

to sunbathe on top of the waves,
that its horned mouth might hoover my hair,
floating like the trailing stings of jellyfish —
I'd have been frightened witless.

Now it's swimming through time and this quiet museum,
round the back of those treasure rooms gleaming with gold
that awe and amaze in Kildare Street.
Croziers and chalices; bog bodies; torcs,

fragments of bone in clay urns.
These rooms display the treasure we forget:
seabirds and songbirds, winging the bright air,
furred creatures, scuttling ancient woods and fields.

On Reading Campbell McGrath's Pax Atomica

'. . . whatever species of trees are still inhabited by Dryads'

There's hardly a Dryad left in Ireland.
None to speak of in February — the first lambs
staggering the mud, their moth-eaten dams
losing their coats; no grass, no fodder,
the screech owl patrolling by night.

Survivors have grown vengeful and half savage.
They shape-change, they're the cruel spikes on the blackthorn,
they wring the twisting hands of the young oaks.

One summer they lived in the Judas tree by our gate.
We saw their bones stick out, we heard them laugh.
That was the year it died.

Green Grass, White Chair

Outside the window there's April.
Inside April, a garden.
On the slope of the garden, a white chair.
In the curve of the white chair, your absence.

It stops me — though it's hard to stop in April
when everything is rushing to become.

Frida Kahlo

In Ireland she would wear a velvet dress
and bind blue sloes and ash keys in her hair,
a shawl the pearling grey of our thin skies,
her crowned hair loosened to a tangled fall.

Trailing the wet fields in draggled hems,
the fading colours would soon leach her eyes
of all that black defiance. Feral and rank,
red fox cubs would find cradling in her arms,

magpies would cloak her shoulders on their watch
for necklet-bones to thieve from rotting kills;
fine rain would teach her water, runnels, ruts,
and gift her mud with its dumb, witching suck.

The Inmost Sea

We wait on the curve of the Bay of the Dead
for sight of the sails on the sea,

and the keels run aground in a swashing of stones,
and we're heaped on the wooden decks,

but we rise and climb to the Place of the Dead,
we stretch in the fresh red graves,

fennel and dill line the breath of the wind,
and we sigh for the world that we've left.

Life

Night —
'I'm having a nightmare. In Russia.
It's snowing and nobody likes me.'
I pull my body
tight against his.
'Everyone likes you.
Especially in Russia.'

Morning —
'They didn't.' He spits toothpaste.
'I went back, they still didn't like me.'
I'm searching the drawer
for two socks the same.
Outside the window
the first frost of Autumn.

Undone

A debris of pocked gold lies on the grass —
strewn garments, rumpled from their tented drape
of summer's sumptuous body, gone to ground.
Grey lace of frost, grey smoke of mist,
the rat's long, slate-grey tail
that drags the gnaw of winter home
to feed the ravening dark.

Acknowledgements and Notes

Acknowledgements are due to the editors of the following publications where some of these poems, or versions of them, were published first: *Axion, Blackbird, The Church Mouse, Heat, The Hospital's Trust Menu, The Irish Times, Magma, The Manchester Review, Northwords Now, La Paume Ouverte: A Festschrift for Françoise Connolly, The Poet Project, Revival, Rialto, Shine On, Southword, The Stinging Fly, The Ulster Tatler, What We Found There* and *Women's Work.*

A version of 'Letter from the Old World' appeared in the programme of *Wind-blown Seeds* composed by Nicola Lefanu for the Arcos String Orchestra and their director, John Edward Kelly, 2012.

'Grace' was published in the cover notes of J. S. Bach's *Sonata in C Major* by Maya Homburger and Barry Guy.

page 22   'By Speed's time military campaigns had become a less important cartographic influence than the confiscation of landed property.' — *The Oxford Companion to Irish History*

page 42   'The ocean sunfish is the heaviest known bony fish in the world. Many of the sunfish's various names allude to its flattened shape. Its specific name, "mola", is Latin for "millstone". Its common English name, "sunfish", refers to the animal's habit of sunbathing at the surface of the water. Sunfish live on a diet that consists mainly of jellyfish.'

page 47   The title also refers to the Mediterranean, as described by G. K. Chesterton in 'Lepanto': '. . . the inmost sea of all the earth is shaken with his ships'.